OUR ROYAL FAMILY

COOMBE BOOKS

The British Royal Family that we know today can trace its roots back to Cerdic, a Saxon warrior who stormed his way onto the southern coast of Britain in AD 495, eventually becoming King of Wessex. One of his descendants, Egbert, King of the West Saxons from 802 to 839, managed to unite most of the disparate kingdoms in the country and hold them against invaders with his strong sword-arm. This paved the way for the political unification of England about the middle of the tenth century. Today, the Queen is the Sovereign of not only Great Britain and Northern Ireland, but a vast Commonwealth of Nations spanning the globe.

Elizabeth II is the Monarch, yet she is also a wife and mother. She married Prince Philip on 20th November, 1947, four months after persuading her father, King George VI, to let her become engaged to this dashing naval officer. The King was to write to her after the wedding, "I can see that you are sublimely happy with Philip."

Their first child, Prince Charles, Duke of Cornwall, was born on 14th November, 1948. He was followed by a daughter, Princess Anne (born 15th August, 1950). Then there were to be two sons: Prince Andrew (born 19th February, 1960), and Prince Edward (born 10th March, 1964).

The importance of family life to Her Majesty was encapsulated at the time of her silver wedding anniversary when she said: "A marriage begins by joining man and wife together, but this relationship between two people, however deep at the time, needs to develop and mature with the passing years. For that it must be held firm in the web of the family relationships, between parents and children, between grandparents and grandchildren, between cousins, aunts and uncles. If I am asked today what I think about family life after 25 years of marriage I can answer with simplicity and conviction. I am for it."

The House of Windsor has been the name of the Royal Family since 1917, during the First World War. At that time, King George V, who was a member of the German House of Saxe-Coburg-Gotha, proclaimed that all descendants of Queen Victoria in the male line who were also British subjects, should adopt the name "of Windsor". Elizabeth II declared, soon after her accession in 1952, that the name was to be used for all her descendants bearing the title of royal highness, prince or princess. Then, on 8th February, 1960, this was modified so that all other descendants were to bear the name of Mountbatten-Windsor, utilising her father's adopted surname.

All members of the Royal Family are personalities in their own right. The Queen Mother is everybody's favourite grandmother. She only became Queen by the unusual circumstance of the abdication of Edward VIII. However, at the age of seven a gipsy woman had held her palm and told her she would be a queen!

Prince Philip is both genial and outspoken. He is a strong-willed father and husband, but in public ensures that he is seen only as the consort of the Queen. She in turn, is well known for her speeches in which she places him first: "My husband and I". He is a fond and loving husband, and is also one of the greatest supporters of the Commonwealth.

Charles is always loved by the crowds, and this was especially so on 29th July, 1981, the day that he took the hand of the young and beautiful Lady Diana Spencer, making her both beloved wife and Princess of Wales. Now their first son, William, has drawn them even more admirers.

Prince Andrew seems to have stolen the headlines recently for his amorous exploits. But it was he who represented the Royal Family when the Task Force sailed for the Falkland Islands, where he flew helicopters for the Fleet Air Arm. Following a State Banquet at Windsor Castle, the Queen, obviously concerned for her son, condemned the Argentinians for their "naked aggression" which had once more plunged Britain unexpectedly into war.

Recently, Prince Edward is coming more to the fore. He will be going into the tough life of the Royal Marines after University; a break from the family tradition of the Royal Navy. His sister, Princess Anne, is a tireless worker for the Riding for the Disabled Association and the Save The Children Fund, of which she is president.

The Royal Family is a well-known and loved institution. There are now many members, all helping to share the burden that must ultimately fall upon the Monarch. There is Princess Margaret, Captain Mark Phillips, the Duke and Duchess of Kent, Princess Alexandra, and the Duke and Duchess of Gloucester. They are all part of an ancient family, enmeshed within a glorious tapestry of history, surrounded by the most colourful pomp and pageantry. As long as Britons thrive under the benevolent rule of a democratic monarchy, so will there be the Royal Family to guide and sustain them through the years ahead.

Each member of our Royal Family
represents the institution of
monarchy. In Tuvalu (left).

Prince Philip is one of the busiest of the royals. Between returning from Canada on 11th November, 1982, and leaving for Geneva on 5th December, he went to almost forty engagements, including (left) awarding certificates as President of the National Playing Fields Association. Princess Anne is well-known for her love of horses and visited the H.Q. of the King's Troop Royal Horse Artillery (this page).

In 1983, on the 28th March, the Prince and Princess of Wales arrived in Sydney and were driven to the Opera House (this page) for an open air programme of dance and music put on by local schools. The forecourt of the Opera House was packed with ten thousand people, many of whom had bought colourful plastic flags for one dollar each. Just before Christmas 1982, there was a photo-call for the six-month-old Prince William (opposite page). The Princess chose to wear a red dress with a low square-cut neckline and frilly blouse for the occasion.

The Queen Mother is everbody's much-loved grandmother and is a frequent guest of honour. On 10th May, 1983, she went to the Royal Anglian Regiment for a visit. The weather proved less welcoming than her hosts: as she began her inspection of the six guards of honour, a sudden

downpour threatened to spoil the occasion, but she happily continued (top left). Later, she watched a parade (left) and toured Meeanee and Hyderabad Barracks (above and opposite page, bottom right). Six weeks later she went to Northern Ireland, amid tight security, for the 75th anniversary of the Territorial Army's presence there. The Queen Mother, who could easily have justified staying at home, displayed both personal courage and confidence in the arrangements that were made for her safety.

There were several bomb scares, but this failed to deter her. In fact, she went through her schedule in an easy and relaxed manner, almost as if she were in the familiar surroundings of her own back garden. In this way she honoured her hosts, encouraged the local community and won for herself universal praise for her unselfish attitude in putting royal duty before her own welfare. But then, her whole life has been lived in this manner.

Prince Andrew is stereotyped as a man with an eye for beautiful girls and the tabloid press loses no opportunity to report his liaisons. On 24th June, 1983, he was able to help honour the memory of the late Lord Mountbatten when he opened the new Mountbatten Centre sports complex at Portsmouth. Prince Andrew's cousins Lord and Lady Romsey were there (right hand pictures). (Overleaf) the Royal Family watch an RAF fly past after the Trooping the Colour ceremony.

In New Zealand Prince Charles met the Maori challenge of a thrown down stick (opposite), picking it up as a sign of friendship. Another ritual was the art of nose-rubbing.

Queen Elizabeth received a horse called Valentine, to add to her already impressive royal stables (left). Prince Claus missed some engagements because of illness, but all was smiles (right) on their farewell.

There were eight members of the Royal Family at Westminster Pier on 16th November, 1982. They were there to welcome Queen Beatrix and Prince Claus of the Netherlands for a four-day State visit, arriving by the ceremonial barge *Royal Nore* from Greenwich, where they were met by the Prince of Wales. Later, there was the customary exchange of gifts.

Perhaps the most prestigious diplomatic event of February 1982 was the Ambassadorial Ball Soirée Francaise held on 22nd February at Grosvenor House in aid of UNICEF and the United Nations Association. The royal guest was the Duchess of Gloucester (this page) who looked radiant, as always. The distinguished company included the patrons of honour, one of whom was Eric Morecambe. His presence was obviously enjoyed by the Duchess (top pictures).

One event each year that Princess Margaret (opposite page) rarely misses is the Royal Caledonian Ball, which was held on the 16th May, 1983, at the Grosvenor House Hotel. One month previously, a new biography of the Princess was written by an old admirer of hers – Christopher Warwick. It appeared to be very much a reflection of the Princess' own account of events that have run through her controversial and eventful life.

Prince Philip (opposite page) always attends at least part of Cowes Week every year. On 1st August, 1982, he competed for the major award in the Royal Southampton Yacht Club's opening regatta – the Queen's Cup. At the helm of the Yeoman class yacht, he crossed the finishing line only 90 seconds behind the winning craft, *Highland Fling*. Two days later, he left for Balmoral.

On 8th August, 1982, the North Wales Shooting School held a celebrity challenge shooting match organised by champion racing driver Jackie Stewart. One team represented the aristocrats and was named *The Lords*. Another, formed from royalty, was called *The Team*. In the last round, when speed was essential, the latter made use of their ladies to load new cartridges, ensuring success. Lord Lichfield (left) looked glum, but the royals (above) celebrated with champagne.

The Prince and Princess of Wales held a photo-session with Prince William (previous pages) in Auckland, New Zealand, in April 1983. The latest member of the Royal Family crawled almost as soon as they put him down on the mat and showed a few of his seven teeth. Prince Charles (this page) loves to play polo, seen with the Queen (above), and is a member of two teams – Maple Leaf and Les Diables Bleus. Among the visitors to the Royal Show on 6th July, 1982, was the Duchess of Gloucester (opposite page). Her visit came just before she celebrated her tenth wedding anniversary.

On 25th May, 1983, at Smith's Lawn, Charles won a medal and his team – Maple Leaf – won a cup (bottom left). However, his wife was again the centre of attention, wearing casual but stylish pedal-pushers. The Prince was in action once more (right) on 29th May, competing in the opening tournament of the Queen's Cup.

The royal couple toured parts of Queensland on 12th April, 1983 (opposite page). Then, before leaving Australia, young Prince William was shown off at Melbourne airport (this page).

The Queen and Prince Philip arrived in Victoria, British Columbia, on 8th March, 1983, on board *Britannia* (opposite page, below) where they gave a reception for members of the press. Their engagements included tea at Royal Roads Military College, where 250 cadets (opposite page, top) provided the guard of honour. In June, the Princess of Wales opened the Royal Preston Hospital (this page) and met many of the patients.

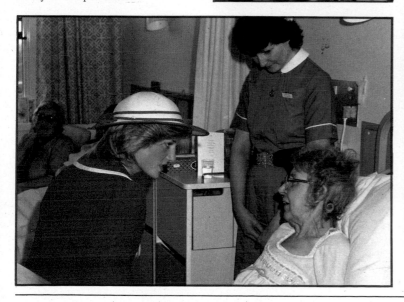

Prince Philip (opposite page) is a keen competitor and took part in the Carriage Driving Grand Prix in May 1983, having won the event the year before. (Above) after church service on the Badminton estate. (Overleaf) glittering occasions during the Australasian tour.

At their annual chapter, held on 13th June, 1983, three more Knights of the Most Noble Order of the Garter were installed (overleaf). After lunch, the service of the Order took place in St George's Chapel, Windsor. In the rear of the slow-moving, but very impressive procession to the Chapel were the Queen, Prince Philip, the Prince of Wales and the Queen Mother.

The Queen's Flight is based at RAF Benson and it was here that Prince Edward gained his glider pilot's wings in 1980. On 12th January, 1983, it was visited (opposite page) by Princess Alexandra. The Princess of Wales (this page) was in Devon on 9th March, seen here meeting the people of Tavistock.

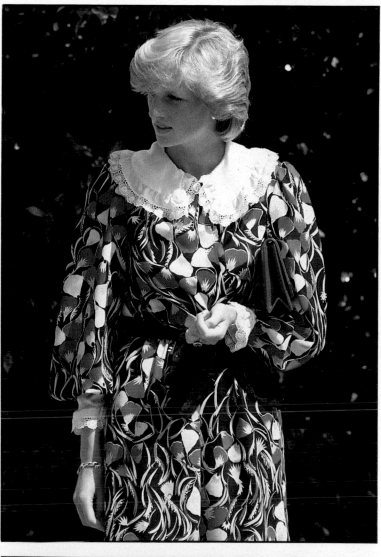

The Prince of Wales was the centre of controversy when, on 6th December, 1982, he joined the Quorn hunt (opposite) near Melton Mowbray. His wife (this page) visited two centres for handicapped children in May 1983, after returning from Australasia.

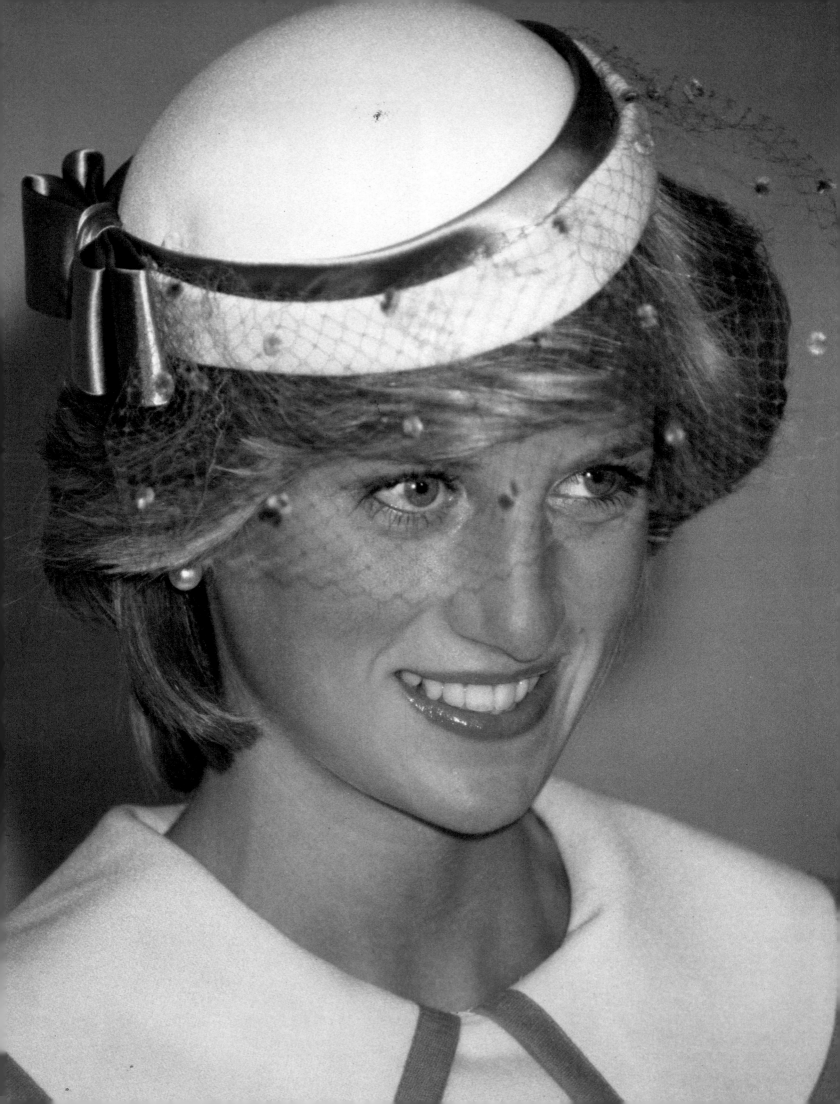

In the same month, Diana visited Canterbury (opposite) where she opened a housing scheme for the elderly and infirm. The Queen Mother (above) opened a hospice on her sixtieth wedding anniversary – 26th April, 1983. The Queen attended a service (below) at Westminster Abbey, on 9th May, marking the centenary of the Co-operative Women's Guild. (Below left) Her Majesty at the opening of the National Horse Racing Museum, Newmarket.

At the International Air Show, Biggin Hill, on 14th May, Prince Andrew (opposite page) arrived at the controls of a Wessex helicopter. Princess Anne attended the Royal Windsor Horse Show (this page) with her two children, Peter and Zara. The Queen was also there to see Prince Philip compete in the Carriage Driving Grand Prix. Although he had won the event in 1982, this year he only managed fourth with his team of Cleveland and Dutch bays.

The Princess of Wales looked particularly radiant when she and her husband drove in an open-topped car (these pages) through the Cornish town of St Columb, which was celebrating the 650th anniversary of King Edward III's charter. Prince Charles, the Duke of Cornwall, was given a book about British trees, published in 1906 and dedicated to King Edward VII.

Britannia arrived in Vancouver harbour on 9th March. There was a walkabout at the University of British Columbia, a tour of the Museum, a visit to the Asian centre and to the site of Expo '86. The Queen (opposite page) received a tumultuous welcome. (This page) exotic Kandy, in Sri Lanka, played host to the Queen and Prince Philip in October 1981. Massive, decorative wickerwork archways welcomed her arrival and a civic reception (top right) was held. Here the Queen was presented with a jewelled brooch, which included a navaratne – a jewel of nine gems, said to ward off the ill-effects of planetary activity.

The Prince of Wales (opposite) in the ceremonial costume of a Knight of the Most Noble Order of the Garter. The motto of the Order can be seen in the photograph: "Honi soit qui mal y pense" – evil be to him who evil thinks. These were the words of King Edward III as he stooped to pick up a lady's garter which had fallen while she was dancing. (This page) the Princess of Wales visiting Brookfields School for Mentally Handicapped Children.

Duty called Prince Andrew, and many others, to war in the South Atlantic. When his ship, *Invincible*, returned to Portsmouth there was a joyous celebration. After a private reunion with his mother there were photographs taken on one of the ship's decks (above). The Prince took the press over to his helicopter (right) and posed with his comrades (far right). Of the war itself he said, "I felt lonely more than anything else". But he knows how to have fun too, indulging in some innocent horse-play with Charles (opposite page).

In April 1983, the Queen Mother (this page) visited Brixton, which had been the scene of bitter riots only two years previously. She came to open a day centre for elderly West Indians and despite persistent rain she walked along Railton Road – the 'Front Line' – where the worst of the troubles had occurred. A large and happy crowd greeted her there.

Princess Michael (previous pages, left) at a concert given by the London Philharmonic Orchestra in Whitehall. In Auckland, the Princess of Wales (previous pages, right) wore a light, loose blouse in a striking black-and-white pattern for a garden party at Government House. She went to the annual Mountbatten concert on 3rd February, 1983 (opposite page), in aid of the Malcolm Sargent Cancer Fund for children, of which she is patron. Her lilac evening dress was much admired.

For their first night out in New Zealand, the royal couple went to see *Coppelia* at St James Theatre (this page). (Opposite) visiting a school in Tennant Creek, Australia.

The members of our Royal Family epitomise the pomp and pageantry associated with the institution of monarchy. All of them have a fine sense of duty to their Sovereign Queen and to their country. They have an important ambassadorial role in promoting Britain and its values to the rest of the world.

First published in Great Britain by Colour Library Books Ltd.
© 1983 Illustrations: Keystone Press Agency, London.
© 1983 Text: Colour Library Books, Guildford, Surrey, England.
Display and text filmsetting by Acesetters Ltd., Richmond, Surrey, England.
Printed and bound in Barcelona, Spain.
All rights reserved.
ISBN 0 86283 115 6

D.L.B. 34 294-83